From Sketchbook
To Linoprint

by Graham Firth

Introduction

I was once asked to write a brief CV to be included
in the prospectus for the college where I worked.
So, I wrote: -

1956 ......Born Doncaster
1957 ......Began drawing
2015 ......Still drawing

It was not well received, so I expanded it into the reworked CV which is at the back of
this book. But what I wrote is essentially true; I have never stopped drawing. In 2002
I decided to monitor my drawing more closely and began to draw every day in an A5
sketchbook and date each page. The drawings could be of anything; either imaginary
doodles, observed drawings or little paintings. My main field of art is printmaking, and
the hope was that from these pages of drawings ideas would emerge that could be
somehow develop into prints.
This book aims to show how a print evolves from a simple idea to a completed image.

A Fistful of Loyalty Cards

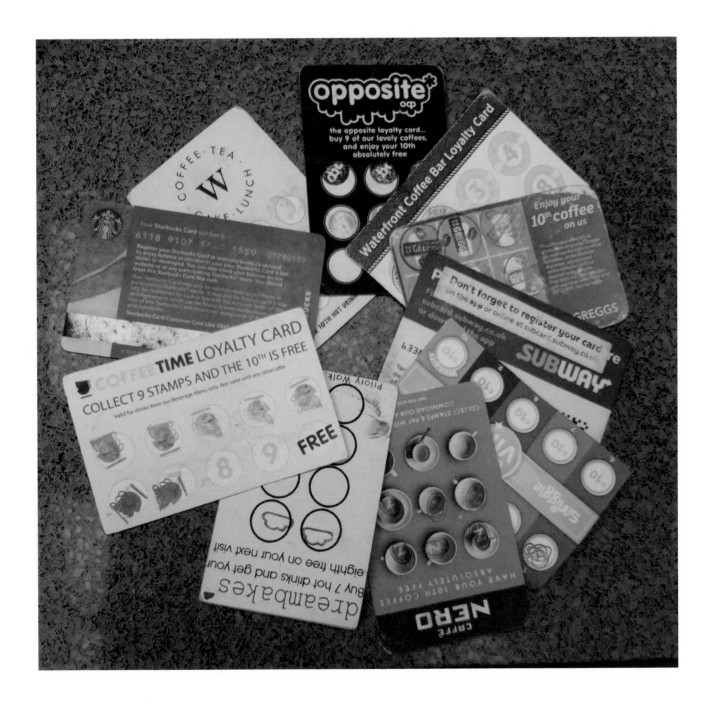

My shed/studio

My shed in winter, warming my inking sheet on a radiator

My hand-built press made from reclaimed wood from a 1930s house renovation. The design was copied from a Youtube video posted by an American printer who had made his press from steel. Underneath the cross bar on this press, and not visible from this view, is a piece of angle iron to strengthen the wood.

The yellow object is a carjack, the top of which fits into a 30mm spanner socket. This is to prevent the jack from slipping. This jack is designed to lift 4 tonnes, so is well able to cope with printing lino and a piece of paper.

Drying racks with added cat

My bag and contents, 18th September 2020

These objects were taken on a drawing expedition my favourite café on Friday 18th September. Not all items were used, but I am a belt and braces type of person. The contents of the bag vary depending on the drawing task to hand.

List of items from my bag, 18th September 2020

Many readers will be familiar with some of the art equipment items listed opposite, but I will list them anyway to clarify.

TOP ROW.
SKETCHBOOK, good quality drawing cartridge paper,150gsm
   not so good for watercolours
MOBILE PHONE
BALLPOINT PENS, 9, in a variety of widths and colours
OVAL WOODEN BOX in 2 halves
Left hand side contains a variety of brush pens, flesh tones and greys
Right hand side, 6 bottles of drawing inks, all different colours and dip pens
NB The box was made by my daughter

MIDDLE ROW
MARKER PENS Set of 24, water-based, bought from a cheap shop,
always a good place to source unusual coloured pens
2 BULLDOG CLIPS small size
GLASS JAR of water

BOTTOM ROW
BUNCH OF KEYS
COMPASS
PLASTIC KNIFE
ELASTAPLAST (actually a cheaper alternative)
PEN KNIFE which includes knife, fork and spoon (Poundshop bargain)
SCISSORS
TORCH
COMBINATION MULTI-TOOL
PROPELLING PENCIL and LEADS, HB
WATER COLOURS, artist quality

This is the drawing completed on Friday 18ᵗʰ September 2020. If I am intending to do a watercolour painting in a session in my favourite café, I usually start with a drawing as this gives me the chance to loosen up. Drawing on the spot is never easy; I have been doing it for forty plus years, and still have trouble getting started. Days vary, some sessions progress rapidly and fluently, this one did not. I began in the top left-hand corner drawing an invalid carriage as there were few people around, this settled me down and eventually I tackled a few of the people milling around. Moving people are difficult to draw, often I will begin drawing one character and get part of their figure down, and then take elements from another passerby and add them to the first. The end result is a hybrid person.

As the session progressed the pen flowed more freely and after forty-five minutes, I had a rest. I then turned the page, drank more tea, and prepared for a watercolour session.

This is the watercolour painting completed on location on Friday 18th September 2020. The paper in the sketchbook is not ideal for the purpose, genuine watercolour paper is more absorbent, but I like the challenge. I have tackled this scene several times in recent weeks in my sketchbook and am convinced that a linoprint version is a possibility. This is the fourth painting in the series, as I need to get a body of drawings and colour studies together to formulate a print. I was most interested in the colour of the characters' clothing and the background items in the shops. I tried to paint each part of the figure in one go, to be as spontaneous as I could manage. So, the legs or trousers being one colour were attempted in as few strokes as possible. The jacket or shirt which would be another colour, was also rendered in a similar manner. The idea was to produce the picture with a limited number of strokes. If it is a failure, then it is just a sheet of paper spoiled but learnt from.

All images in this book have been made by the author. The drawing above and the strip below have been reproduced from my sketchbook as have many more that you will see throughout the book. I use my sketchbooks every day and from them I get the inspiration for my linoprints. This book aims to show you how my ideas develop.

My sketch books

The dictionary definition of a sketch is that it is a quick rough drawing. Therefore, a sketchbook is a book full of such drawings. I do not totally agree with this as many of my sketchbook pages are much more detailed.

About my sketchbooks

They are nearly all A5 in size. They are dated and numbered on the spine and arranged in order on shelves in my shed/workshop. They are for reference. They are not all the same brand but come from a variety of sources. The important thing for me is that they are good quality and robust. They take a lot of hammer and are portable; able to fit into a pocket or small bag. It takes about 3 months to fill one. If they are left without a distinctive cover, they can become mixed up. In the past I have taken the wrong sketchbook out with me, and that can be disappointing. I simply paste a favourite image onto the plain cover.

Most of my sketchbook work is done on the spot, in cafes or on beaches on holiday. A normal session is at least an hour long, and then continues at home. The drawings are completed or added to days or months later. I constantly re-visit the sketchbooks. I have made prints that were inspired by drawings from sketchbooks produced years earlier.

I work in my sketchbooks every night, seated on the floor, next to the television, surrounded by art equipment. I either add to the drawing that began that day, or sort through previous sketchbooks looking for inspirations for linoprints.

This is a typical sketchbook double page spread, begun on the spot from a vantage point similar to the position illustrated on the previous page but one. All the figures will have been drawn in the one session, and some of the colours will have been inked in. As can be seen, I take a wide selection of equipment with me, including ball point and marker pens.

A note on the words around the edges of the sketchbook page:

Each page is dated. Around the edge of the page there are often notes referring to world events, the state of the weather or family birthdays; usually quite trivial things. The sketchbooks have turned into a series of diaries, but they are not necessarily 100% accurate. I often write down things like 'such and such d. 86', which means ' such and such has died aged 86,' but I write this down when I first hear of it, I may be a day or two out, and it may be the wrong age, but it is intended to be accurate.

Also, when I draw in a café, I cover the whole double page spread with the picture, consequently I am usually in front of myself. So, if a picture is dated 16th February 2010, it may have been drawn three' days after that date, I hope that this is clear. I date the pages to monitor myself and make sure I am not slacking.

Some sketchbook pages look like this after the first session, sometimes they are left like this, but more often than not they are finished off at home, either in my shed or in the front room, whilst watching the television at night. It can be the same day, or it could be weeks or months later. There is always a pile of old sketchbooks in the front room. I go through them all the time, looking for any scrap of a page that could be turned into a print.

This is a small collection of my marker pens. They come from a variety of manufacturers, both cheap and expensive. I have one set of pens in the front room under the coffee table next to where I sit on the floor .The box of pens in the phot is in my shed and is arranged in a sort of spectrum so that I don't have to sort through looking for a specific pen. To the left- hand side of this tray there is a row of flesh and brown coloured pens, and to the right all the grey and black pens. When I am drawing on the spot, I take a much more limited range, usually some greys, flesh coloured pens and a set of primary colours. I fill in the unusual colours first. For instance, if a person has purple hair that goes in straight away; if I have forgotten the purple pen I will write on the drawing 'purple hair', so as not to forget. I rarely finish a sketchbook drawing in one go in situ.

My Studio work desk

This drawing was made using marker pens on the beach in Lyme Regis in Dorset whilst on holiday. It was begun on the spot on the beach and completed later. I take my sketchbook everywhere and have drawings of dozens of different beaches. I prefer crowds, but I will also have a go at landscapes, cliffs, rocks, and boulders, whatever is there.

I like to use a double-page spread format, and for that reason I never buy spiral bound sketch books, because it is difficult to work around the central spring. There is also a centimetre gap of nothing in the centre of the drawing.

I take my sketchbook with me virtually everywhere I go, just in case an unexpected situation arises that could make an interesting drawing. This situation is a case in point. How often do you see a great crowd of policemen doing absolutely nothing? They were expecting a possible influx of troublesome football supporters on the next train. There was a pre-season friendly scheduled that afternoon, and these same supporters had caused trouble the previous week in a neighbouring town.

   I was struck by the strong shapes the figures made, and the limited range of colours. The policemen could be rendered in dark blue, lemon yellow and grey for their uniforms, and flesh colour for their skin. This is perfect for a linoprint, and a few weeks later a print was begun.

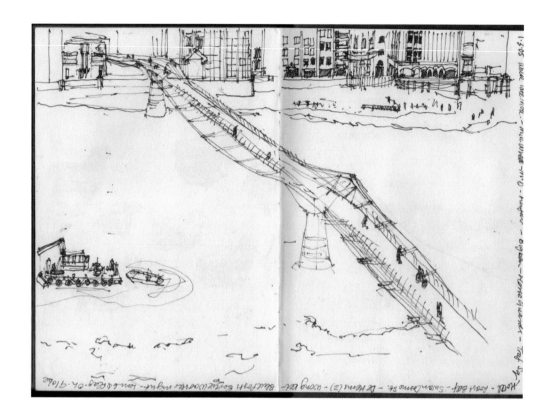

Above is the original sketch drawn from the café of the Tate Modern, London. Below are some compositional sketches from a week or two afterwards.

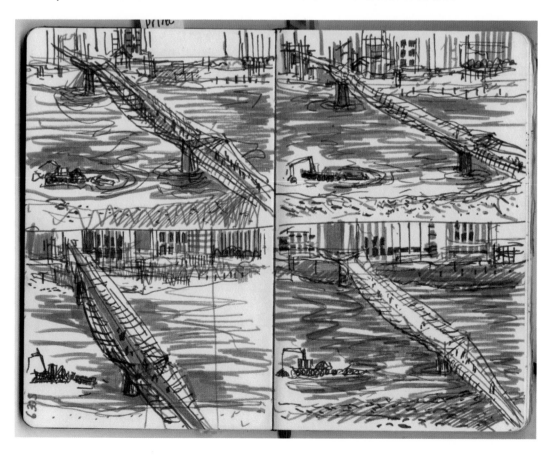

The sketches on the opposite page show a variety of different compositions, but there were many more pages. In some sketches the frames of the pictures were in the portrait format. There were drawings in a variety of different media, in monotone and colour, and after all that effort, I settled on a design which was almost the same as the first drawing. In this linoprint, the main difference is that I moved the dredging boat fractionally to the left, and added a row of streetlights and banners, one of which has the date and my initials carved into it.

Meadowhall shopping centre in Sheffield was the venue for this drawing. I was seated in a vantage point overlooking a large communal eating area at the end of one of the malls. A ballpoint pen was used to draw most of the figures and tables. This is a very rapid drawing tool, dries instantly and does not smudge. The drawing was begun in the bottom left-hand corner and gradually spread across the page in all directions. I had taken a limited selection of brush-pens with me, several shades of flesh, some greys, and a couple of bright colours and filled in the relevant areas on the spot. I soon realized that this was a definite print and made several more trips to establish the colour schemes of the floor and tables. All the drawings were photocopied twice each, cut up, manipulated, and glued onto pieces of card to make collages. These were later painted using a limited range of colours. The best one was used as the basis for the linoprint. Seven colours or less is ideal for a print.

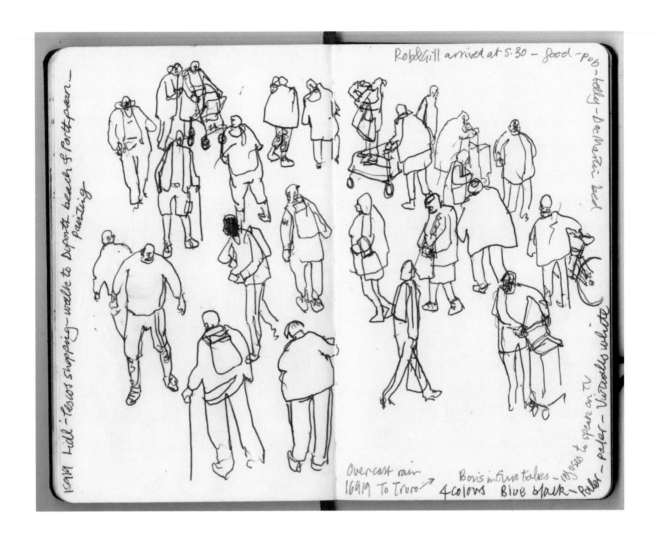

The drawing was made using a ballpoint pen with 1.6mm ball in the drawing point. Most pen points are below 1 mm in diameter. The advantage of this pen is that as well as making a very wide line the ink absolutely floods out and makes for very quick spontaneous drawing. It is also possible to achieve a range of tones by varying the amount of pressure applied when drawing. This is another study made from the upper floor of my favourite café, and it was one of those rare occasions when everything seemed to go right. It was as if the pen had taken over. Again, this drawing became a print with virtually no alterations. This book may be giving the impression that my sketchbooks are full of successful drawings that easily transfer into linoprints, but that is misleading. Some sketchbooks produce no linoprints, and they run to about one hundred pages. The harder I try to find ideas for a print, the less chance I seem to have of finding any inspiration.

Occasionally I try to make something happen by taking a different approach. In this I case randomly filled in every area with the first colour that came to hand. Water based marker pens were used to complete this drawing. It was begun on location; I attempted to draw every person that walked by in as few lines as possible using a fine line marker. I began in the top left-hand corner, working from left to right, a bit like a typewriter. The colouring in was done at home seated on the floor surrounded by pens whilst watching the television. It was an enjoyable session, but nothing resulted from it.

Ideas development; Mick the Multitasker

I am now going to describe how the drawing above became the linoprint below

My sketchbooks are filled with pages like the one below. They are probably confusing to the viewer, so I will explain. This is a double page spread. The left- hand page is a working sketch for a linoprint that I was working on at the time; the areas filled in with green are the parts of the lino that are to be removed. This is the first stage of this print, and these areas will appear white on the print i.e. they are the colour of the paper. On the right-hand panel there is a lot of writing, one part is a proposed list of the colours to be used in the linoprint. To the right of the list is a circle of letters; this is my attempt to solve an anagram in a crossword. Then there is a line across, then it says PRINTS and a list of three print ideas. To the right of that it says Bampton - Downton; this is where the TV programme Downton Abbey is filmed; I must have looked it up. Most importantly there is a tiny drawing of a man on a bike, and this would eventually become a linoprint. It was also my 59th birthday.

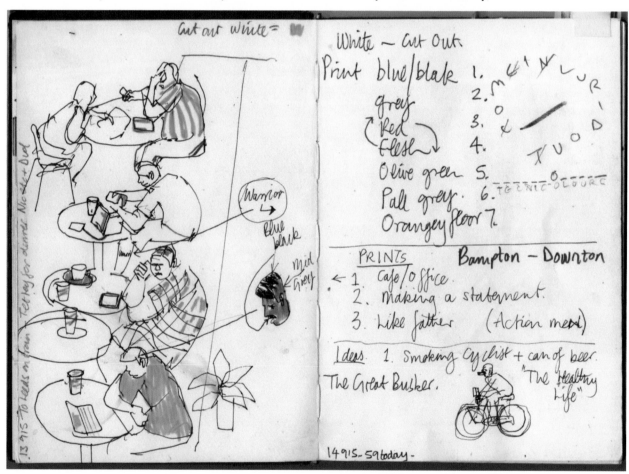

I was seated in a café with my sketchbook open looking at the drawing of my latest linoprint, trying to work out the running order of its colours. I noticed a man go by several times on a bike. I was struck by his nonchalance and dexterity as he effortlessly pedaled his bike, smoked a cigarette, held a can of beer, and texted simultaneously. This was real multitasking!

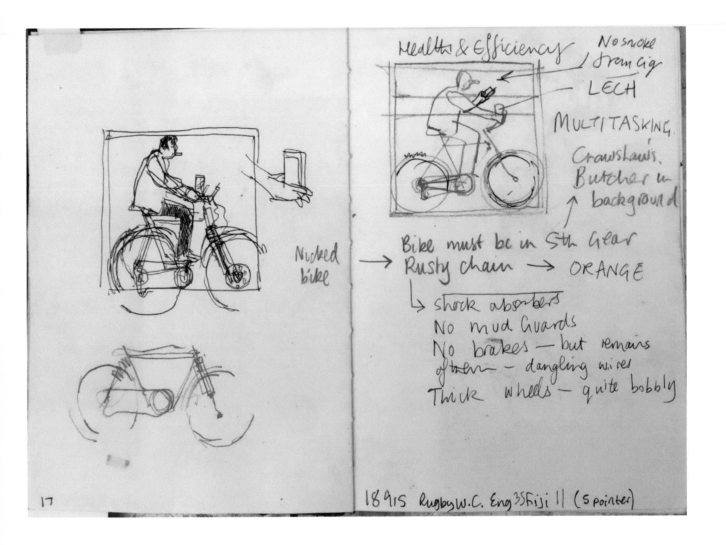

Health & Efficiency   No smoke
                           from cig

LECH

MULTITASKING.

Crawshaw's.
Butcher in
background

Nicked
bike

Bike must be in 5th Gear
Rusty chain → ORANGE
↳ shock absorbers
No mud Guards
No brakes — but remains
of them — dangling wires
Thick wheels — quite bobbly

17

18 915 Rugby W.C. Eng 35 Fiji 11 (5 pointer)

Four days later I realized that this was a potential print and went back to town to draw bikes and men capable of multitasking. On the left- hand page is a further drawing with a square drawn around it; this first idea was to show only part of the bike. There is also a drawing of a hand holding a can of beer. I was puzzled. How do you grip a can and steer at the same time? On the right-hand page is a lot of writing where I am attempting to describe what I remember about the bike that I saw. It was a rusty bike, stuck in 5th gear, no brakes or mud guards but intriguingly it had shock absorbers. The cyclist had a can of Lech strong beer in one hand. The word Multitasking is written in capitals; this is the first mention of this idea, although the future print has not been officially titled. Also, it says 'Health and Efficiency', which was the title of a naturist magazine from the 1960s, which is not appropriate.

The next appearance in my sketchbook of this print development is about three weeks later, and I am still working on the hand positions. I am trying to draw the hands in as few lines as possible, as they must be strong simple shapes. 'The cyclist is now more hunched over. In the intervening three weeks I would have been working on another print and doing my real job, i.e. working.

Around the edge of the page there are mentions of news stories of the day. The recurrent theme of the cyclist somehow fitting into a square appears again here, and finally I realized that the whole bike should fit in the box.

Three weeks later we are back to square one, using one of the first ideas. This is an enlargement, and it is obvious that the man's face, hands, clothing, and bike have still to be resolved. I never saw the original cyclist again, therefore a lot of research was required. I would have to sit in the cafe drinking tea and looking out for similar cyclists.

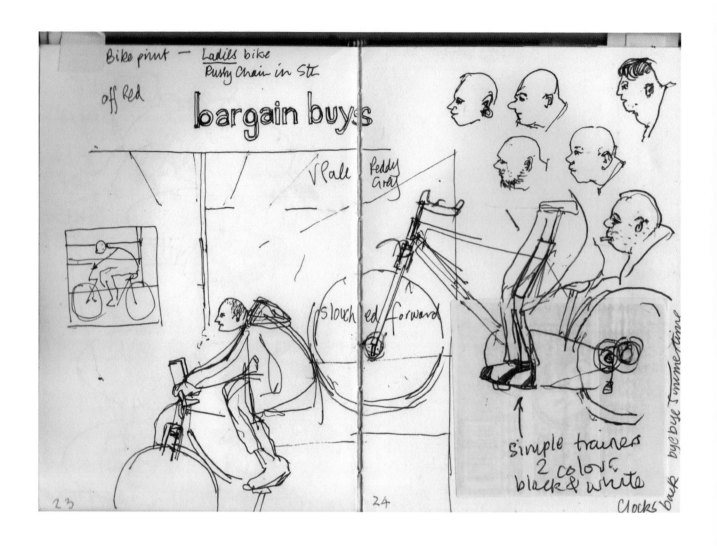

Also, I had to draw some genuine bikes as accurately as possible. It occurred to me that if the rider was on a lady's bike without a crossbar, then the bike shape would be simpler still, and if the chain was stuck in 5th gear, the angle of the chain would be optically pleasing.

I was developing the posture of the rider emphasising the slouch and the protruding neck and firm set jaw. This bloke was really concentrating. I drew several similar men, eventually setting on a bald chap with a bit of stubble, and the odd large pimple.

On the following pages are more studies of bikes and hands, and lots of written comments.

This bike looks too professional →

Make it simpler

Ladies bike — better without cross bar

Down a bit

More or less flat tires version 1

To kings kynn Beer of Europe — Then Stamford Lines

28 1015 VV Wet To. work print Colours

Snape Suzy.

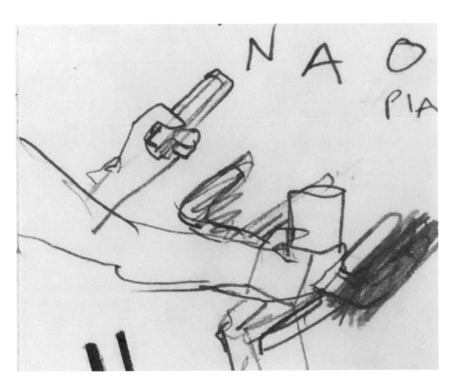

N A O
PIA

Even though the shape of the cyclist and his bike are almost sorted, I still thought that it could be improved. I went to town again to draw some genuine cyclists, paying particular attention to their leg positions and clothing. In the bottom righthand corner there is a mention of a particular item of clothing; tracksuit bottoms with blue stripes that only reach to the knees, a small detail but it balances well with the bike frame. On the opposite page is a new version.

make poll'd orange

A TOO BROWN

LEC

CNA

TY

STE

30.10.15 Wet Start

Cafe offia finished

— Suzy back to heads & stein caravan hol —

This is the first coloured attempt in my sketchbook, and it is nearly resolved. The colours are too murky and the lettering in the top strip is distracting, so will eventually be discarded.

This is the final design, and remarkably close to the Master Drawing. The shape of the image would not now change throughout the print production, but there would be some more alterations to the colour scheme. This image was next photocopied and manipulated to the correct size for the lino, was printed out on photocopy paper and glued to a piece of thick card.

This is the absolute final image, correct in shape and colour, and will be referred to throughout as the Master Drawing. It is the same size as the linoprint will be, and the colours for each stage of printing must be mixed as closely as possible to these on this painting. Some areas have been overpainted with gouache. The middle strip is much brighter than the previous version, whereas the floor and the hoody top are darker than before, but I think it is sharper and simpler.

The lino must be prepared before it is ready for use. For this print I used the thickest lino that I could find at 4.1 mm. It was stuck onto a piece of 8mm plywood with wood glue and placed onto the printing press, and weighted down and left for a couple of hours to dry. This is to keep it perfectly flat so that it does not warp or deform. When large areas of lino are removed the overall shape can shrink unless it is mounted, and this can make it difficult to line up with the previous colours. This lino has a surface treatment on it to protect it from scratches, and this must be removed with methylated spirits and wire wool to make it smooth to minimize the texture produced when printed.

Transferring the image onto the lino can now begin. The first stage is to produce a fully accurate tracing of the Master Drawing. Both the Master and the tracing paper are secured to the work surface with masking tape so they cannot move, and an outline is inscribed around every part of the drawing with an exceptionally fine line pen.

The tracing paper is then turned over and placed over the lino. It is turned over because all images print backwards. Both lino and tracing paper are taped to the desktop so that they cannot move. The lino is secured at each corner, and the tracing paper along one edge, so that it can be folded back to check progress. Between the tracing paper and the lino a sheet of carbon paper is inserted. The image is then over traced using a ballpoint pen and it appears on the lino. The carbon paper does not have to stay in the same place, it can be moved around by simply folding back the tracing paper and rearranging it.

When the tracing is finished a blue picture appears on the lino, this is then overdrawn with a permanent marker so that it can only be removed with methylated spirits. It cannot be removed with white spirit or cooking oil. This is important as this will be a reduction linoprint, meaning the same piece of lino is used throughout the process, and the picture must not be erased.

I must stress here that this is the complicated way I produce linoprints. It may seem long and drawn out; but I do not know any other way; and it works for me, most of the time.

Red   1. Blue Black   4. Blue
       2. Red   5. Rusty Brown
       3. Flesh   6. Grey

6. Grey
= Cut out WHITE

cig smoke   MADE
             RESEARCH
             A S O S R
               E H E

New Order
1 Black Black
2. Blue.
3. Red. 4. Flesh. 5 Rusty Br. 6. Grey

3·11·15

In my sketchbook I then draw a quick version of the print, copying from the lino opposite. I must decide which areas to remove. I fill them in in pink in my sketchbook. These areas will appear white on the finished print, they are the colour of the paper. I then copy these areas onto the lino with a marker pen, and the cutting begins.

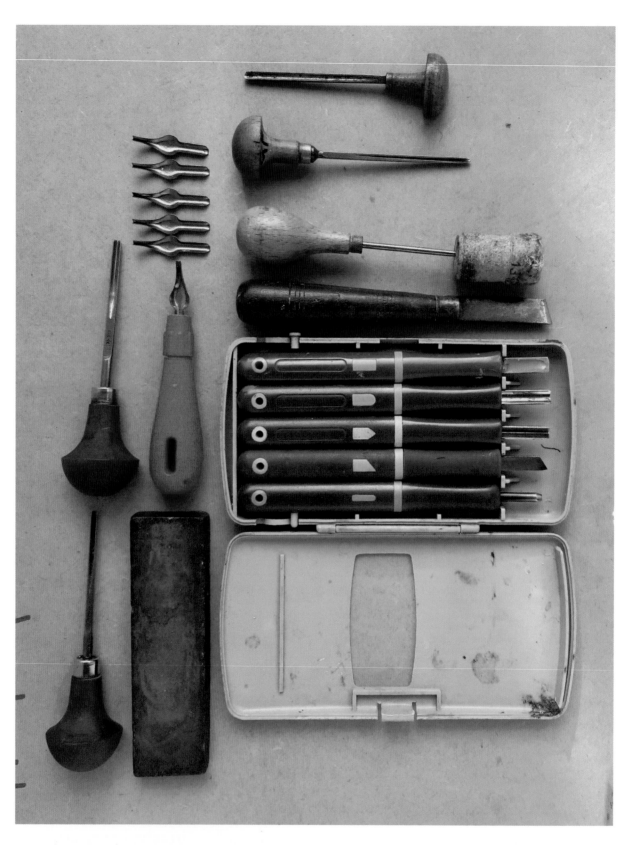

This is my collection of lino cutting tools. At the top and down the left-hand side are wooden handled wood engraving tools, all with different width cutting edges, very sharp and excellent for lino cutting. The red handled tool has detachable blades, which are arranged above it.

In the grey box is a set of Japanese woodcutters, and there is a sharpening stone and a very sharp needle for making dotty holes. The cork is a safety measure. It is a type of awl for making holes in leather, but I use it for making dots in pictures. I used it in the featured print for making spots on the cyclist's head. If you force the needle into the lino and then squiggle it around a bit you can churn the lino surface into a sort of mini volcano, which can be quite effective.

Below are two vital tools: on the left is the finer of my wood engraving tools, and on the right is a wire brush. I have several wood engraving tools and they all have wooden handles. They are used by holding the handle in the palm of your hand with the pointed end held firmly by the fingers. You then push forward removing the lino smoothly. These tools are used in areas of fine detail.

The wire brush may be a surprise to some people; a toothbrush or a nail brush can be used to do the same job. It is used to clear the lino chippings from the cut out areas. Bits of lino that break off during printing make dots on finished prints as they get picked up by the roller and prevent even distribution of the ink onto the lino. So, a good scrub with a stiff brush of the lino is always the last thing to be done before inking commences.

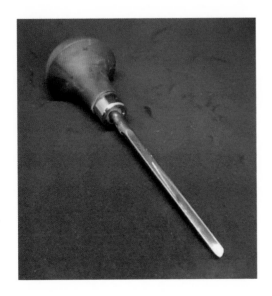

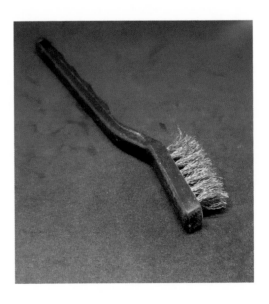

These Japanese tools are particularly useful. They are not designed for exceptionally fine cutting; but for removing large areas of wood or lino. The tool on the left is a V-shaped cutter and will produce a mid-width line. The second and fourth tools are cutting knives and are used to cut straight down into the lino to delineate areas to be removed with the remaining two gouges. If you cut around the edge of an area to be removed, and then cut up to this line with a gouge, the lino will snap off cleanly.

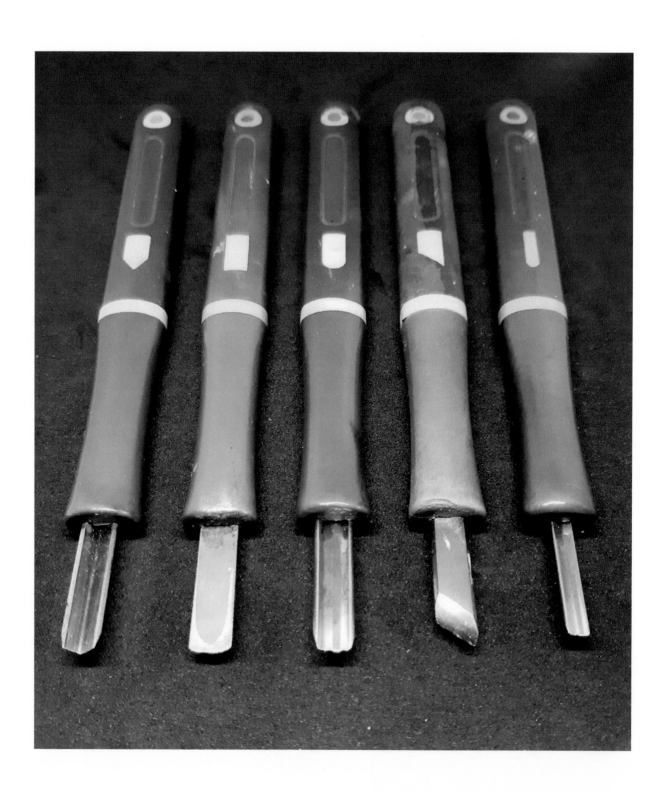

I am using a wood cutting tool here with the handle held firmly in the palm of my hand with only the very sharp pointed end protruding. The sharper the point, the cleaner the cut. 'Always point the tool away from the body', is the Health and Safety advice. These tools are obviously very sharp, or they would not do the job. Care is needed, if you push too hard the tool can shoot away from you and plough a furrow where it is not required.

I almost always use oil-based inks which are supplied in metal tubes, metal tins and in recent years, plastic cartridges. This ink is very thick when removed from the tin with a spatula, and it does not run off the blade. In the past, skin forming on the surface of ink in tins was a big problem, as it had to be removed to reach the useable stuff. Therefore, there was a lot of waste. Some manufacturers have stopped including drying agents in the inks, and now you must buy a chemical called 'Driers' in small bottles and add it to the ink just before use. The two types I have used are Manganese .and Cobalt driers, and I add eight to ten drops for a print run of twelve. The ink is then usually dry within 24 hours.

To mix the ink I have a collection of knives and spatulas. The important thing is that they have springy flexible blades which aids the mixing process. Knives from painting and decorating suppliers are usually much cheaper than those from printmaking specialists.

I have a sheet of toughened glass on which to mix and roll out my ink. After printing all rollers must be cleaned with either white spirit or cooking oil, which is a greener alternative. The roller, which is the most expensive item, is washed with washing up liquid afterwards to remove all traces of cooking oil or white spirit, to keep it in pristine condition.

Mixing enough ink for an edition of 12 is not easy. When I say an edition of 12 this is misleading, as I usually print 14, not 13 as that is unlucky. I use the extra 2 prints to try colour experiments on. Back to the point, trial and error is the only way you will learn how much ink is needed for your edition, err on the side of too much, as colour matching extra ink is not easy.

It is vital to keep to the colours used on the Master Drawing. This will be a 6-colour reduction print, and the colours must be matched exactly. The order of printing has been decided, the first colour Is a bluey black and during the mixing process the colour is dabbed onto the blue-black areas on the Master Drawing to achieve an exact match. When ready the roller can be brought into use.

This is a 30cm wide, 5cm thick, soft green plastic roller. It is perfect for rolling out large areas of colour. The ink is applied to the whole length of the roller in a 1cm wide strip using a pallet knife. It is then rolled out onto the glass to the correct thickness. This is something else which requires trial and error. The ink should look velvety when rolled out, and the roller should make a hissing sound on the glass. If the ink is the correct thickness on the glass it will be the correct thickness when rolled onto the lino. If it is too thick it will have small waves in it, and when applied to the lino it will spread and fill in any finely detailed areas.

WHAT IS A REDUCTION LINOPRINT?

A reduction linoprint is a print that is completed in several colours using the same piece of lino throughout. The image is drawn onto the lino with indelible ink, all areas that will appear white on the print are removed. The first colour is applied to the lino and this is printed onto all twelve sheets of paper. The lino is then cleaned and dried and all areas that are to remain the first colour are removed. The second colour is printed onto the twelve sheets of paper, and on and on. All will be revealed as the book progresses.

Inking can now commence. The illustration below shows the author inking the lino which has been glued onto a sheet of plywood. This is necessary when producing a reduction linoprint, because in this method the same piece of lino is used throughout. As more and more of the lino is cut, away unless it is stuck to a board, it can warp, distort, or shrink making it difficult to register.

WHAT IS REGISTRATION?

Registration is the process by which all colours line up on top of each other on the finished print. This is a difficult process. Some printers simply place the lino on top of each sheet of paper manually. This is not easy, and can result in fingerprints appearing on the edges of prints where they should not be.

My solution is to use a registration plate, sometimes called a jig. The registration plate is adapted for each print run and has been used many times. It is simply a piece of thick plywood which acts as a base. Around the bottom edge and down the right-hand side two thin strips of wood, called lats, have been nailed. The inked-up lino is then placed against these two lats. There are also two lats on the opposite corners for the paper to butt against. The lino is always placed in the same place after each inking, and the paper always placed against the opposite lats.

A great deal of care and attention is needed to ensure that the paper is placed against the registration lats neatly. Both leading edges must touch the two lats. This is not easy, but this very thick paper known as Somerset Satin stays rigid throughout the complete print process.

Some thinner papers can begin to curl and deform after several sets of colours have been printed, and this can affect the registration. Once in place the paper is gently smoothed onto the lino so that it will not move when placing the registration board under the press.

This is my homemade press as described in detail at the beginning of this book. The car jack is resting on a pyramid shaped press block, which has been made from six layers of plywood all glued together. Underneath that is the registration board which sits on the thick base of the press. The whole press is bolted together with lengths of 10mm threaded bar, cut to size and secured with nuts and washers.

The registration board, with the lino and paper in place, is positioned on the press as close as possible to the middle. The side of the board has been measured and marked with an arrow to show the mid-point. It is important that the lino is exactly in the middle of the press to get an even impression. The next two photos show the layers of packing which are placed on top of the paper. First is a double layer of etching press felt, followed by twenty sheets of newsprint and finally a sheet of cardboard. This combination was arrived at after much trial and error.

On top of the packing is placed a block of plywood boards which looks like a pyramid. This is made of the same gauge plywood as the registration board, and just fits inside the base of the press. Each layer of the pyramid is 5cm smaller than the previous one and is all glued together to make a solid block, seven layers in total. A car jack is placed on top of the block, this is held in place by a socket from a spanner set to stop it from slipping. When the car jack is tightened the pressure it exerts is evenly spread by the pyramid construction. I initially made a four-level pyramid but it did not produce an even image.

I usually leave the print underneath the press for a few seconds before releasing the pressure on the car jack. I then carefully remove the pyramid and the packing, take the registration plate out of the press, and slowly peal back the print, checking to see if there are any flaws in the ink coverage. If for any reason there are missed areas of printing, I place the paper back down and roll on the back with a special heavy-duty steel roller that I obtained from a vinyl floor installers supplier. The roller can be seen to the left of the registration plate. This usually smooths out misprints. The first colour of a new print often appears patchy on the paper. This could be because the lino is not uniformly smooth; the paper may have texture variations; or the printer may be at fault with his rolling technique.

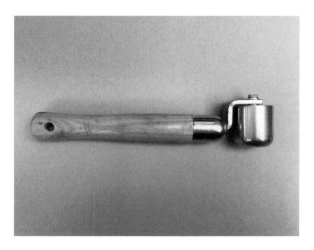

Here it is, Colour one printed onto fourteen separate sheets of Somerset Satin, all the same size, perfectly registered, hopefully. The first print is often fainter than subsequent copies as the lino is not yet fully loaded with ink. The Master Drawing is used to colour match the inks. When the ink is mixed a small sample is taken on a finger and dabbed onto the Master to see if it is the same colour. When the colour is matched perfectly the dabbed area should be difficult to see because it should be the same colour. This can take a while, as can be seen on the Master for this print a few pages after this one.

Colour 2 appears a bit dotty in the middle section, but this area will not be maroon in the final print, and the subsequent layers of ink should fill in over the top. All areas to remain blue-black have been removed and red-maroon has been rolled onto the lino.

The finished print in an edition of twelve. As close as possible in colour to the Master Drawing, and it only took about twelve weeks. The prints are later numbered in pencil in the bottom left-hand corner on the clean paper, in order. The first is numbered 1/12, the next is 2/12 and so on.

This is the lino at the end of the process, coated in the final colour. The lino has been cut very deeply, as can be seen by the shadows in the wheel sections.

At the end of the print run, the Master Drawing is covered in fingerprints, which show how much difficulty I had in matching colours. The average time to mix the correct colour is about 20 minutes, unless it is a straightforward 'Out of the tin' colour which rarely happens.

'Mick the Multitasker' has only one subject, and that is a man riding a bicycle, but that is not how I normally work. Most of my linoprints have several people in them. In fact I have produced quite a few artworks that involve crowds of people. To produce a crowd type picture takes a different approach, I call it the collage system. In this way of working I think of an idea for a linoprint based on some drawings, work out a basic design, and then photocopy several pages, cut them up and make a collage. Sounds easy, but it is time consuming.

I decided that I wanted to produce a linoprint in a 'portrait' format, that is a vertical format rather than a horizontal layout. I had an idea of the setting of the print, so I spent a couple of weeks drawing from the same spot and completed a large group of sketches in my book.

The pages were then photocopied at 100%, and then at 105, 110, and 115%, two pages of each, so I had a great pile to choose from, and they were then cut up and rearranged on several large sheet of paper to make pleasing compositions. They were reproduced in a variety of sizes, so that a sense of depth could be created in the final design. If all the figures are the same size, then the picture could look a bit flat. Over the next pages most, but not all, of the sketchbook pages have been reproduced. On odd occasions, instead of drawing in my sketchbook in the normal format, I have turned the book on its side to draw across the pages in a portrait mode, so these pages will be bigger than life size.

The idea for the print began around the 1st September 2010, about the time I would be expected to resume teaching at the art department at my local college. Six weeks later I was arriving at the first stages of the final design. Between those two dates are many duff drawings, failed ideas and printing dead ends. These are not the only drawings I did in that time frame; they have been edited to give some idea of my thought process. On the following pages are two views of myself at work on location in the café overlooking the crowd scene.

5 silly hats run in a family

Eng 12 Aug 9 league day drawings + windy 10.9.11

11.9.11 Anniv of 9/11 Windy

8.2.11 Soltaire Brow 9 visit Sal 6 tastes, sauv + cheese — drawing in current + students

Rem split

2.3.11 Talk at Rotterdam 7-9 Slow market in current again

Cern — Neutrins break Speed of light!

8.9.11 ladies day sol packed

9.9.11 Hot Rugby W. Cup open NZ

4

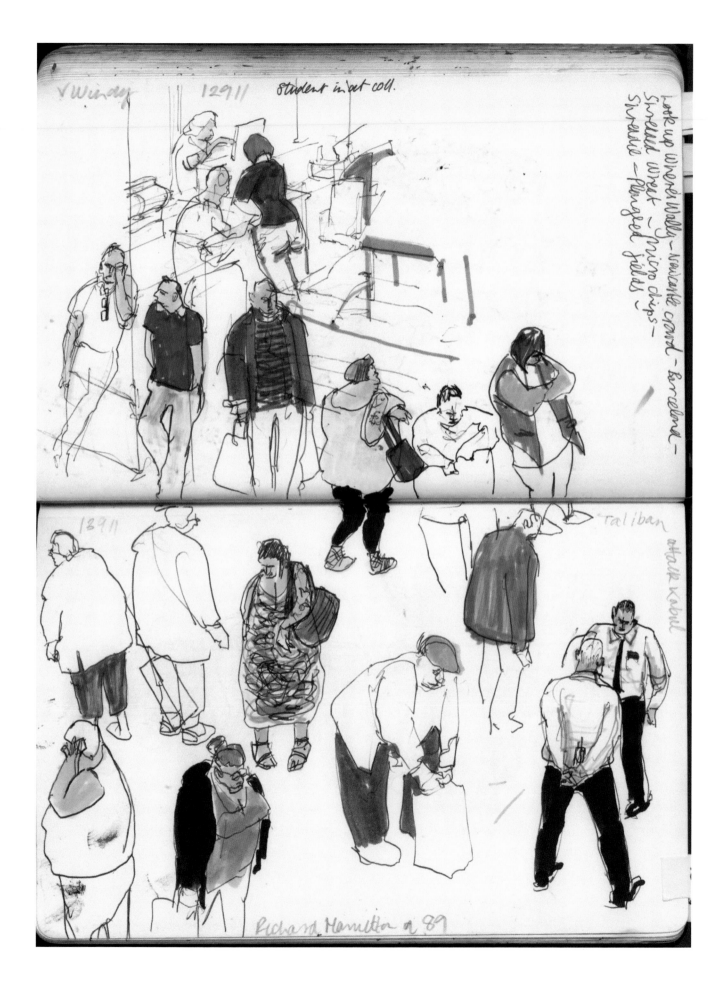

Windy   12911   student in'art coll.

Look up Wrene Walls ~ Newcastle crowd ~ Barcelona ~
Sheeld Wreck ~ micro chips ~
Shreshe ~ Plunged fields ~

12911

Taliban
attack Kabul

Richard Hamilton a 89

1494 Mehanny us may momoo David rang from S fransisco

1591 Sal Girell in trouble - Euro struggling   S Wales Coal mine 4 missing

At this point all of the pages to be used for the print had been photocopied. The most interesting figures were drawn quickly and placed randomly on the right-hand half of the double page layout above, in an attempt to jumpstart the creative process. On the left-hand page is a list of name ideas for future prints, most of which never happened. The title sometimes comes first but is not always used. This print was originally titled 'From Pillar to Post', but ended up entitled, 'Eyes Right'. Interestingly, number ten on the list, 'Donkey Brown's Art Class', was finally printed in 2020 and she can be seen scuttling along the bottom of this page.

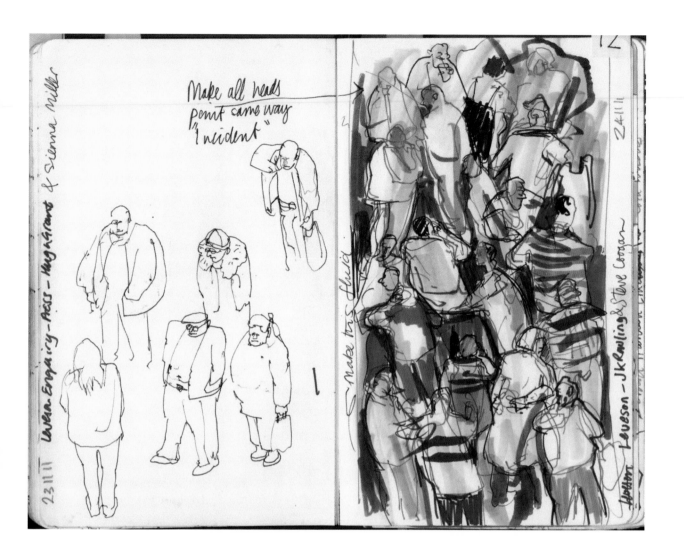

Ten days later a new method is introduced. This involved drawing another version of the crowd and rearranging the figures. Instead of a linear treatment, a limited range of colour has been employed using marker pens. Seven colours or less are preferable for a linoprint. The colours are chosen from the previous sketchbook photocopies.

The subsequent pages show the metamorphosis of the print. These are all on A4 paper, and if you look closely it is possible to see layers of paper on top of each other. I use white sticky envelope labels which come on a roll. They always stick and can be painted over with gouache paint or marker pens. I spend far more time looking at these pictures than drawing on them. I leave the sketchbook page open, leant up where I can see it, while I watch television until I realize the adjustments to be made.

Use these Colour but other figures

Here is the Master Drawing, which is unusually in a A4 sketchbook,
rather than mounted on a piece of card. Many figures have been replaced or
reconfigured, and the one character who is facing to the left has gradually moved up
the picture frame until she is towards the middle of the picture. On the right-hand
page is a list of the colours to be used in the final print, and a small study of three
figures showing the final fine-tuning of the composition.
The background colour was a big problem and was overpainted several times with
different colours before a satisfactory colour was achieved.
On the next page is the finished item, printed in an edition of twelve.

In the last two years I have expanded my sketchbook repertoire by purchasing a small I-pad and Pencil and entered the world of digital media. I draw on location on my I-pad and continue at home in the same way as in my paper sketchbook. The app I use is Procreate, and I find it is easy to work with, and versatile.

I combine my digital way of working with paper-based work. I photograph my more interesting sketchbook pages with my I-pad, download the image onto Procreate, and colour it in and add lines to it with my Apple Pencil. I am going to finish this book with some of my digital sketches. They are all interior views of the cafes I frequent. Some of these drawings have been added to many times, and are still not resolved. I thought it might be of interest to see the view of the café rather than the view from the café.

Coffee Time Downstairs

Coffee Time near Argos

Donuts

Waterstones

Dunkin2

Starbucks featuring Luca and Courtney

Starbucks 2

Starbucks3

Starbucks 4

Waterstones upstairs.

Corner Costa

Dunkin Again.

I do not consider any of the café interior drawings to be finished. The advantage of working with an I-pad is that it is easily portable and versatile. It is a simple task to erase large areas and redraw as many times as required, and that is how I operate. If I cannot find a suitable seat to draw out of the café, I simply get out my I-pad and draw inwards.

In all my long experience of drawing in cafes and bars I have never been asked to leave; told to hurry up and finish; or molested in any way by members of staff or management; and for this and their excellent service I thank them.

GRAHAM FIRTH

The author began his artistic career at Doncaster School of Art in 1976, had a brief spell at Winchester College of Art studying Fine Art, before transferring to Manchester Polytechnic to continue his degree. He entered the college's print room one day and remained there for the next two and a half years, graduating in 1979 with a BA (Hons) in Fine Art (Printmaking). The next eight years were spent working for British Rail as a Rope Splicer/Blacksmiths' Striker and General Labourer. Afterwards he spent several years as a part-time teacher, working in everything from infant schools, teaching ceramics to the children's mothers, to teaching painting in care homes and everything in between .Included in this period were three years at HMP Lindholme teaching ceramics, painting and graphic design. Eventually he returned to Doncaster College and spent the next thirty years in the print room. He taught at every stage from Level 1 Art and Design to BA Art. He left in 2018 and has spent the interim in his shed printing, and in coffee shops, drawing.

He has exhibited widely in Britain and in some parts of Europe.

grahamfirth28@hotmail.com   **firth.graham on instagram**

The cafes that are featured in this book are as follows: -

COFFEE TIME (both branches)
STARBUCKS
DUNKIN (DONUTS)
COSTA, corner branch
COSTA, in Waterstones
SUBWAY

All the above are in the Frenchgate Centre, Doncaster, South Yorkshire.

Also featured are the following venues in Doncaster

DREAMBAKES
COSTA, Baxtergate branch
SCICLUNNA'S DELI
DEREK'S CAFÉ in Doncaster Corn Exchange

My thanks go out to all of these venues and the people who work in them, and I hope they all continue to prosper.

I would also like to thank my wife Rose for helping me set this book up and for proofreading it. A big thank you also to Neil McGregor, Belinda Pollit, Liz Salter, Barbara Johnson and Cathy Tuson for pointing out and correcting my numerous punctuation errors and spelling mistakes.